This Prayer Journal Belongs to

_____

How to Use This Prayer Journal

This is an undated 13-week prayer journal focusing on the names of God. Each week begins with a particular Name of God. Write the scripture reference in which the name is found in your favorite version, or maybe even more than one version.

Talk with God about what the name says to you. Write those thoughts as they come to mind.

Begin the next day with a scripture reference from your own reading plan. **Before you start reading** the scripture, ask God, through the Holy Spirit, to illuminate the scripture so that your understanding of Him, His Word, and His will for your life will grow ever deeper.

The song, Open My Eyes That I May See," has a refrain that is repeated in every verse with a slight variation from eyes, to ears, to heart. This makes an excellent prayer for hearing from God:
"Silently now I wait for thee,
Ready, my God, thy will to see.
Open my eyes, illumine me, Spirit divine!"

Next, ask God how this scripture relates to your life right now, and how He wants you to respond to what He has revealed..

During your meditation, God may bring people to mind that He wants you to reach out to in some way. Write their names and how you sense God wants you to respond.

There are additional lines to write anything else God says to you.

My prayer is that as you develop a daily quiet time with the Lord, Psalm 42:1-2 becomes very real to you "As a deer longs for flowing streams, so I long for you, God. I thirst for God, the living God. When can I come and appear before God?" CSB

El Roi – The God Who Sees Me

Genesis 16:13-14

What this Name of God says to me

Date _____

Scripture _____

_____
_____
_____
_____
_____

What word or phrase speaks to my heart?

_____
_____
_____

God, how does this relate to my life right now?

_____
_____
_____
_____
_____

God, what do you want me to do in response?

_____
_____
_____
_____
_____
_____
_____

People God brought to my mind today

_____
_____
_____
_____
_____

Additional thoughts

_____
_____
_____
_____

Date _____

Scripture _____

_____
_____
_____
_____
_____

What word or phrase speaks to my heart?

_____
_____
_____

God, how does this relate to my life right now?

_____
_____
_____
_____
_____

God, what do you want me to do in response?

_____
_____
_____
_____
_____
_____

People God brought to my mind today

_____
_____
_____
_____

Additional thoughts

_____
_____
_____
_____

Date _____

Scripture _____

_____
_____
_____
_____
_____

What word or phrase speaks to my heart?

_____
_____
_____

God, how does this relate to my life right now?

_____
_____
_____
_____
_____

God, what do you want me to do in response?

_____
_____
_____
_____
_____
_____

People God brought to my mind today

_____
_____
_____
_____

Additional thoughts

_____
_____
_____
_____

Date _____

Scripture _____

_____
_____
_____
_____
_____

What word or phrase speaks to my heart?

_____
_____
_____
_____

God, how does this relate to my life right now?

_____
_____
_____
_____
_____

God, what do you want me to do in response?

_____
_____
_____
_____
_____
_____
_____

People God brought to my mind today

_____
_____
_____
_____

Additional thoughts

_____
_____
_____
_____

Date _____

Scripture _____

_____
_____
_____
_____
_____
_____

What word or phrase speaks to my heart?

_____
_____
_____
_____

God, how does this relate to my life right now?

_____
_____
_____
_____
_____

God, what do you want me to do in response?

_____
_____
_____
_____
_____
_____
_____

People God brought to my mind today

_____
_____
_____
_____
_____

Additional thoughts

_____
_____
_____
_____

El Shaddai – God Almighty

Genesis 35:11

What this Name of God says to me

Date

Scripture

What word or phrase speaks to my heart?

God, how does this relate to my life right now?

God, what do you want me to do in response?

_____
_____
_____
_____
_____
_____
_____

People God brought to my mind today

_____
_____
_____
_____
_____

Additional thoughts

_____
_____
_____
_____

Date

Scripture

What word or phrase speaks to my heart?

God, how does this relate to my life right now?

God, what do you want me to do in response?

_____
_____
_____
_____
_____
_____
_____

People God brought to my mind today

_____
_____
_____
_____

Additional thoughts

_____
_____
_____
_____

Date

Scripture

What word or phrase speaks to my heart?

God, how does this relate to my life right now?

God, what do you want me to do in response?

_____
_____
_____
_____
_____
_____
_____

People God brought to my mind today

_____
_____
_____
_____
_____

Additional thoughts

_____
_____
_____
_____

Date

Scripture

_____
_____
_____
_____
_____

What word or phrase speaks to my heart?

_____
_____
_____

God, how does this relate to my life right now?

_____
_____
_____
_____

God, what do you want me to do in response?

_____
_____
_____
_____
_____
_____
_____

People God brought to my mind today

_____
_____
_____
_____

Additional thoughts

_____
_____
_____
_____

Date _____

Scripture _____

_____
_____
_____
_____
_____

What word or phrase speaks to my heart?

_____
_____
_____

God, how does this relate to my life right now?

_____
_____
_____
_____

God, what do you want me to do in response?

_____
_____
_____
_____
_____
_____
_____

People God brought to my mind today

_____
_____
_____
_____
_____

Additional thoughts

_____
_____
_____
_____

El Yeshuati – The God of My Salvation
Isaiah 12:2

What this Name of God says to me

Date _____

Scripture _____

_____
_____
_____
_____
_____

What word or phrase speaks to my heart?

_____
_____
_____
_____

God, how does this relate to my life right now?

_____
_____
_____
_____
_____

God, what do you want me to do in response?

_____
_____
_____
_____
_____
_____
_____

People God brought to my mind today

_____
_____
_____
_____
_____

Additional thoughts

_____
_____
_____
_____

Date _____

Scripture _____

_____
_____
_____
_____
_____

What word or phrase speaks to my heart?

_____
_____
_____

God, how does this relate to my life right now?

_____
_____
_____
_____
_____

God, what do you want me to do in response?

_____
_____
_____
_____
_____
_____
_____

People God brought to my mind today

_____
_____
_____
_____
_____

Additional thoughts

_____
_____
_____
_____

Date _____

Scripture _____

_____
_____
_____
_____
_____

What word or phrase speaks to my heart?

_____
_____
_____

God, how does this relate to my life right now?

_____
_____
_____
_____
_____

God, what do you want me to do in response?

_____
_____
_____
_____
_____
_____
_____

People God brought to my mind today

_____
_____
_____
_____
_____

Additional thoughts

_____
_____
_____
_____

Date _____

Scripture _____

_____
_____
_____
_____
_____

What word or phrase speaks to my heart?

_____
_____
_____
_____

God, how does this relate to my life right now?

_____
_____
_____
_____
_____

God, what do you want me to do in response?

_____
_____
_____
_____
_____
_____
_____

People God brought to my mind today

_____
_____
_____
_____

Additional thoughts

_____
_____
_____
_____

Date _____

Scripture _____

_____
_____
_____
_____
_____

What word or phrase speaks to my heart?

_____
_____
_____

God, how does this relate to my life right now?

_____
_____
_____
_____
_____

God, what do you want me to do in response?

_____
_____
_____
_____
_____
_____
_____

People God brought to my mind today

_____
_____
_____
_____
_____

Additional thoughts

_____
_____
_____
_____

El Yisrael – The God Of Israel

Psalm 68:35

What this Name of God says to me

Date _____

Scripture _____

_____
_____
_____
_____
_____

What word or phrase speaks to my heart?

_____
_____
_____

God, how does this relate to my life right now?

_____
_____
_____
_____
_____

God, what do you want me to do in response?

_____
_____
_____
_____
_____
_____
_____

People God brought to my mind today

_____
_____
_____
_____
_____

Additional thoughts

_____
_____
_____
_____

Date _____

Scripture _____

_____
_____
_____
_____
_____

What word or phrase speaks to my heart?

_____
_____
_____
_____

God, how does this relate to my life right now?

_____
_____
_____
_____
_____

God, what do you want me to do in response?

_____
_____
_____
_____
_____
_____
_____

People God brought to my mind today

_____
_____
_____
_____
_____

Additional thoughts

_____
_____
_____
_____

Date _____

Scripture _____

_____
_____
_____
_____
_____

What word or phrase speaks to my heart?

_____
_____
_____

God, how does this relate to my life right now?

_____
_____
_____
_____
_____

God, what do you want me to do in response?

_____
_____
_____
_____
_____
_____
_____

People God brought to my mind today

_____
_____
_____
_____

Additional thoughts

_____
_____
_____
_____

Date _____

Scripture _____

_____
_____
_____
_____
_____
_____

What word or phrase speaks to my heart?

_____
_____
_____
_____

God, how does this relate to my life right now?

_____
_____
_____
_____
_____

God, what do you want me to do in response?

_____

_____

_____

_____

_____

_____

People God brought to my mind today

_____

_____

_____

_____

Additional thoughts

_____

_____

_____

_____

Date _____

Scripture _____

_____
_____
_____
_____
_____

What word or phrase speaks to my heart?

_____
_____
_____

God, how does this relate to my life right now?

_____
_____
_____
_____
_____

God, what do you want me to do in response?

_____
_____
_____
_____
_____
_____
_____

People God brought to my mind today

_____
_____
_____
_____
_____

Additional thoughts

_____
_____
_____
_____

Elah Sh'maya – God Of Heaven

Ezra 7:23

What this Name of God says to me

Date _____

Scripture _____

_____
_____
_____
_____
_____

What word or phrase speaks to my heart?

_____
_____
_____

God, how does this relate to my life right now?

_____
_____
_____
_____
_____

God, what do you want me to do in response?

_____
_____
_____
_____
_____
_____
_____

People God brought to my mind today

_____
_____
_____
_____
_____

Additional thoughts

_____
_____
_____
_____

Date

Scripture

_____
_____
_____
_____
_____

What word or phrase speaks to my heart?

_____
_____
_____

God, how does this relate to my life right now?

_____
_____
_____
_____
_____

God, what do you want me to do in response?

_____
_____
_____
_____
_____
_____
_____
_____

People God brought to my mind today

_____
_____
_____
_____
_____

Additional thoughts

_____
_____
_____
_____

Date _____

Scripture _____

_____
_____
_____
_____
_____

What word or phrase speaks to my heart?

_____
_____
_____
_____

God, how does this relate to my life right now?

_____
_____
_____
_____
_____

God, what do you want me to do in response?

_____
_____
_____
_____
_____
_____
_____

People God brought to my mind today

_____
_____
_____
_____
_____

Additional thoughts

_____
_____
_____
_____

Date _____

Scripture _____

_____
_____
_____
_____
_____

What word or phrase speaks to my heart?

_____
_____
_____

God, how does this relate to my life right now?

_____
_____
_____
_____

God, what do you want me to do in response?

_____
_____
_____
_____
_____
_____
_____

People God brought to my mind today

_____
_____
_____
_____

Additional thoughts

_____
_____
_____
_____

Date _____

Scripture _____

_____
_____
_____
_____
_____
_____

What word or phrase speaks to my heart?

_____
_____
_____
_____

God, how does this relate to my life right now?

_____
_____
_____
_____
_____
_____

God, what do you want me to do in response?

_____
_____
_____
_____
_____
_____
_____

People God brought to my mind today

_____
_____
_____
_____

Additional thoughts

_____
_____
_____
_____

Elaḥ Sh'maya V'Araḥ – God of Heaven and Earth

Ezra 5:11

What this Name of God says to me

Date _____

Scripture _____

_____
_____
_____
_____
_____

What word or phrase speaks to my heart?

_____
_____
_____
_____

God, how does this relate to my life right now?

_____
_____
_____
_____
_____

God, what do you want me to do in response?

_____
_____
_____
_____
_____
_____
_____

People God brought to my mind today

_____
_____
_____
_____

Additional thoughts

_____
_____
_____
_____

Date _____

Scripture _____

_____
_____
_____
_____
_____
_____

What word or phrase speaks to my heart?

_____
_____
_____
_____

God, how does this relate to my life right now?

_____
_____
_____
_____
_____

God, what do you want me to do in response?

_____

_____

_____

_____

_____

_____

_____

People God brought to my mind today

_____

_____

_____

_____

Additional thoughts

_____

_____

_____

_____

Date _____

Scripture _____

_____
_____
_____
_____
_____

What word or phrase speaks to my heart?

_____
_____
_____

God, how does this relate to my life right now?

_____
_____
_____
_____
_____

God, what do you want me to do in response?

_____

_____

_____

_____

_____

_____

_____

People God brought to my mind today

_____

_____

_____

_____

_____

Additional thoughts

_____

_____

_____

_____

Date _____

Scripture _____

_____
_____
_____
_____
_____
_____

What word or phrase speaks to my heart?

_____
_____
_____
_____

God, how does this relate to my life right now?

_____
_____
_____
_____
_____

God, what do you want me to do in response?

_____
_____
_____
_____
_____
_____
_____

People God brought to my mind today

_____
_____
_____
_____

Additional thoughts

_____
_____
_____
_____

Date

Scripture

What word or phrase speaks to my heart?

God, how does this relate to my life right now?

God, what do you want me to do in response?

_____

_____

_____

_____

_____

_____

People God brought to my mind today

_____

_____

_____

_____

_____

Additional thoughts

_____

_____

_____

_____

Elah Yerush'lem – God of Jerusalem

Ezra 7:19

What this Name of God says to me

Date

Scripture

What word or phrase speaks to my heart?

God, how does this relate to my life right now?

God, what do you want me to do in response?

_____

_____

_____

_____

_____

_____

_____

People God brought to my mind today

_____

_____

_____

_____

Additional thoughts

_____

_____

_____

_____

Date _____

Scripture _____

_____
_____
_____
_____
_____

What word or phrase speaks to my heart?

_____
_____
_____

God, how does this relate to my life right now?

_____
_____
_____
_____

God, what do you want me to do in response?

_____
_____
_____
_____
_____
_____
_____

People God brought to my mind today

_____
_____
_____
_____

Additional thoughts

_____
_____
_____
_____

Date _____

Scripture _____

_____
_____
_____
_____
_____

What word or phrase speaks to my heart?

_____
_____
_____

God, how does this relate to my life right now?

_____
_____
_____
_____
_____

God, what do you want me to do in response?

_____
_____
_____
_____
_____
_____
_____

People God brought to my mind today

_____
_____
_____
_____
_____

Additional thoughts

_____
_____
_____
_____

Date _____

Scripture _____

_____
_____
_____
_____
_____

What word or phrase speaks to my heart?

_____
_____
_____

God, how does this relate to my life right now?

_____
_____
_____
_____
_____

God, what do you want me to do in response?

_____
_____
_____
_____
_____
_____
_____

People God brought to my mind today

_____
_____
_____
_____

Additional thoughts

_____
_____
_____
_____

Date _____

Scripture _____

_____
_____
_____
_____
_____

What word or phrase speaks to my heart?

_____
_____
_____
_____

God, how does this relate to my life right now?

_____
_____
_____
_____
_____

God, what do you want me to do in response?

_____
_____
_____
_____
_____
_____
_____

People God brought to my mind today

_____
_____
_____
_____
_____

Additional thoughts

_____
_____
_____
_____

Elohim Chaiyim – Living God

Jeremiah 10:10

What this Name of God says to me

Date

Scripture

What word or phrase speaks to my heart?

God, how does this relate to my life right now?

God, what do you want me to do in response?

_____
_____
_____
_____
_____
_____
_____

People God brought to my mind today

_____
_____
_____
_____
_____

Additional thoughts

_____
_____
_____
_____

Date _____

Scripture _____

_____
_____
_____
_____
_____

What word or phrase speaks to my heart?

_____
_____
_____

God, how does this relate to my life right now?

_____
_____
_____
_____
_____

God, what do you want me to do in response?

_____

_____

_____

_____

_____

_____

_____

People God brought to my mind today

_____

_____

_____

_____

_____

Additional thoughts

_____

_____

_____

_____

Date _____

Scripture _____

_____
_____
_____
_____
_____

What word or phrase speaks to my heart?

_____
_____
_____

God, how does this relate to my life right now?

_____
_____
_____
_____
_____

God, what do you want me to do in response?

_____

_____

_____

_____

_____

_____

People God brought to my mind today

_____

_____

_____

_____

Additional thoughts

_____

_____

_____

_____

Date ———————————————

Scripture ———————————————

_____
_____
_____
_____
_____

What word or phrase speaks to my heart?

_____
_____
_____

God, how does this relate to my life right now?

_____
_____
_____
_____

God, what do you want me to do in response?

_____
_____
_____
_____
_____
_____
_____

People God brought to my mind today

_____
_____
_____
_____
_____

Additional thoughts

_____
_____
_____
_____

Date _____

Scripture _____

_____
_____
_____
_____
_____

What word or phrase speaks to my heart?

_____
_____
_____

God, how does this relate to my life right now?

_____
_____
_____
_____
_____

God, what do you want me to do in response?

_____
_____
_____
_____
_____
_____
_____

People God brought to my mind today

_____
_____
_____
_____
_____

Additional thoughts

_____
_____
_____
_____

Elohim Elohim – God of Gods

Deuteronomy 10:17

What this Name of God says to me

Date _____

Scripture _____

_____
_____
_____
_____
_____

What word or phrase speaks to my heart?

_____
_____
_____
_____

God, how does this relate to my life right now?

_____
_____
_____
_____
_____

God, what do you want me to do in response?

_____
_____
_____
_____
_____
_____
_____

People God brought to my mind today

_____
_____
_____
_____
_____

Additional thoughts

_____
_____
_____
_____

Date _____

Scripture _____

_____
_____
_____
_____
_____

What word or phrase speaks to my heart?

_____
_____
_____

God, how does this relate to my life right now?

_____
_____
_____
_____
_____

God, what do you want me to do in response?

_____
_____
_____
_____
_____
_____

People God brought to my mind today

_____
_____
_____
_____

Additional thoughts

_____
_____
_____
_____

Date _____

Scripture _____

_____
_____
_____
_____
_____

What word or phrase speaks to my heart?

_____
_____
_____

God, how does this relate to my life right now?

_____
_____
_____
_____
_____

God, what do you want me to do in response?

_____
_____
_____
_____
_____
_____
_____

People God brought to my mind today

_____
_____
_____
_____
_____

Additional thoughts

_____
_____
_____
_____

Date _____

Scripture _____

_____
_____
_____
_____
_____

What word or phrase speaks to my heart?

_____
_____
_____

God, how does this relate to my life right now?

_____
_____
_____
_____

God, what do you want me to do in response?

_____
_____
_____
_____
_____
_____
_____

People God brought to my mind today

_____
_____
_____
_____
_____

Additional thoughts

_____
_____
_____
_____

Date _____

Scripture _____

_____
_____
_____
_____
_____

What word or phrase speaks to my heart?

_____
_____
_____
_____

God, how does this relate to my life right now?

_____
_____
_____
_____
_____

God, what do you want me to do in response?

_____
_____
_____
_____
_____
_____
_____

People God brought to my mind today

_____
_____
_____
_____
_____

Additional thoughts

_____
_____
_____
_____

Elohim Kedem – God Of The Beginning
Deuteronomy 33:27

What this Name of God says to me

Date

Scripture

What word or phrase speaks to my heart?

God, how does this relate to my life right now?

God, what do you want me to do in response?

_____
_____
_____
_____
_____
_____
_____

People God brought to my mind today

_____
_____
_____
_____
_____

Additional thoughts

_____
_____
_____
_____

Date _____

Scripture _____

_____
_____
_____
_____
_____
_____

What word or phrase speaks to my heart?

_____
_____
_____
_____

God, how does this relate to my life right now?

_____
_____
_____
_____
_____

God, what do you want me to do in response?

_____
_____
_____
_____
_____
_____
_____

People God brought to my mind today

_____
_____
_____
_____

Additional thoughts

_____
_____
_____
_____

Date

Scripture

What word or phrase speaks to my heart?

God, how does this relate to my life right now?

God, what do you want me to do in response?

_____
_____
_____
_____
_____
_____
_____

People God brought to my mind today

_____
_____
_____
_____

Additional thoughts

_____
_____
_____
_____

Date _____

Scripture _____

_____
_____
_____
_____
_____

What word or phrase speaks to my heart?

_____
_____
_____

God, how does this relate to my life right now?

_____
_____
_____
_____
_____

God, what do you want me to do in response?

_____
_____
_____
_____
_____
_____
_____

People God brought to my mind today

_____
_____
_____
_____

Additional thoughts

_____
_____
_____
_____

Date

Scripture

_____
_____
_____
_____
_____

What word or phrase speaks to my heart?

_____
_____
_____

God, how does this relate to my life right now?

_____
_____
_____
_____
_____

God, what do you want me to do in response?

_____
_____
_____
_____
_____
_____
_____

People God brought to my mind today

_____
_____
_____
_____

Additional thoughts

_____
_____
_____
_____

Elohim Kedoshim – Holy God

Leviticus 19:2

What this Name of God says to me

Date _____

Scripture _____

_____
_____
_____
_____
_____

What word or phrase speaks to my heart?

_____
_____
_____

God, how does this relate to my life right now?

_____
_____
_____
_____
_____

God, what do you want me to do in response?

_____
_____
_____
_____
_____
_____
_____

People God brought to my mind today

_____
_____
_____
_____
_____

Additional thoughts

_____
_____
_____
_____

Date _____

Scripture _____

_____
_____
_____
_____
_____

What word or phrase speaks to my heart?

_____
_____
_____

God, how does this relate to my life right now?

_____
_____
_____
_____
_____

God, what do you want me to do in response?

_____
_____
_____
_____
_____
_____

People God brought to my mind today

_____
_____
_____
_____

Additional thoughts

_____
_____
_____
_____

Date _____

Scripture _____

_____
_____
_____
_____
_____

What word or phrase speaks to my heart?

_____
_____
_____

God, how does this relate to my life right now?

_____
_____
_____
_____
_____

God, what do you want me to do in response?

_____
_____
_____
_____
_____
_____
_____

People God brought to my mind today

_____
_____
_____
_____
_____

Additional thoughts

_____
_____
_____
_____

Date _____

Scripture _____

_____
_____
_____
_____
_____

What word or phrase speaks to my heart?

_____
_____
_____
_____

God, how does this relate to my life right now?

_____
_____
_____
_____
_____

God, what do you want me to do in response?

_____
_____
_____
_____
_____
_____
_____

People God brought to my mind today

_____
_____
_____
_____
_____

Additional thoughts

_____
_____
_____
_____

Date ———————————————————

Scripture ——————————————————

_____
_____
_____
_____
_____

What word or phrase speaks to my heart?

_____
_____
_____

God, how does this relate to my life right now?

_____
_____
_____
_____

God, what do you want me to do in response?

_____
_____
_____
_____
_____
_____
_____

People God brought to my mind today

_____
_____
_____
_____

Additional thoughts

_____
_____
_____
_____

Elohim Marom – God of Heights

Micah 6:6

What this Name of God says to me

Date _____

Scripture _____

_____
_____
_____
_____
_____

What word or phrase speaks to my heart?

_____
_____
_____

God, how does this relate to my life right now?

_____
_____
_____
_____
_____

God, what do you want me to do in response?

_____

_____

_____

_____

_____

_____

People God brought to my mind today

_____

_____

_____

_____

_____

Additional thoughts

_____

_____

_____

_____

Date _____

Scripture _____

_____
_____
_____
_____
_____

What word or phrase speaks to my heart?

_____
_____
_____

God, how does this relate to my life right now?

_____
_____
_____
_____
_____

God, what do you want me to do in response?

_____
_____
_____
_____
_____
_____
_____

People God brought to my mind today

_____
_____
_____
_____
_____

Additional thoughts

_____
_____
_____
_____

Date _____

Scripture _____

_____
_____
_____
_____
_____

What word or phrase speaks to my heart?

_____
_____
_____
_____

God, how does this relate to my life right now?

_____
_____
_____
_____
_____

God, what do you want me to do in response?

_____
_____
_____
_____
_____
_____
_____

People God brought to my mind today

_____
_____
_____
_____
_____

Additional thoughts

_____
_____
_____
_____

Date _____

Scripture _____

_____
_____
_____
_____
_____

What word or phrase speaks to my heart?

_____
_____
_____

God, how does this relate to my life right now?

_____
_____
_____
_____

God, what do you want me to do in response?

_____
_____
_____
_____
_____
_____
_____

People God brought to my mind today

_____
_____
_____
_____
_____

Additional thoughts

_____
_____
_____
_____

Date

Scripture

What word or phrase speaks to my heart?

God, how does this relate to my life right now?

God, what do you want me to do in response?

_____
_____
_____
_____
_____
_____
_____

People God brought to my mind today

_____
_____
_____
_____
_____

Additional thoughts

_____
_____
_____
_____

Elohim Mauzi – God Of My Strength
Psalm 43:2

What this Name of God says to me

Date _____

Scripture _____

_____
_____
_____
_____
_____

What word or phrase speaks to my heart?

_____
_____
_____

God, how does this relate to my life right now?

_____
_____
_____
_____
_____

God, what do you want me to do in response?

_____
_____
_____
_____
_____
_____
_____

People God brought to my mind today

_____
_____
_____
_____
_____

Additional thoughts

_____
_____
_____
_____

Date _____

Scripture _____

_____
_____
_____
_____
_____

What word or phrase speaks to my heart?

_____
_____
_____
_____

God, how does this relate to my life right now?

_____
_____
_____
_____
_____

God, what do you want me to do in response?

_____
_____
_____
_____
_____
_____
_____

People God brought to my mind today

_____
_____
_____
_____

Additional thoughts

_____
_____
_____
_____

Date _____

Scripture _____

_____
_____
_____
_____
_____

What word or phrase speaks to my heart?

_____
_____
_____
_____

God, how does this relate to my life right now?

_____
_____
_____
_____
_____

God, what do you want me to do in response?

_____

_____

_____

_____

_____

_____

_____

People God brought to my mind today

_____

_____

_____

_____

Additional thoughts

_____

_____

_____

_____

Date _____

Scripture _____

_____
_____
_____
_____
_____

What word or phrase speaks to my heart?

_____
_____
_____
_____

God, how does this relate to my life right now?

_____
_____
_____
_____
_____

God, what do you want me to do in response?

_____
_____
_____
_____
_____
_____
_____

People God brought to my mind today

_____
_____
_____
_____
_____

Additional thoughts

_____
_____
_____
_____

Date _____

Scripture _____

_____
_____
_____
_____
_____

What word or phrase speaks to my heart?

_____
_____
_____

God, how does this relate to my life right now?

_____
_____
_____
_____

God, what do you want me to do in response?

_____

_____

_____

_____

_____

_____

People God brought to my mind today

_____

_____

_____

_____

Additional thoughts

_____

_____

_____

_____

Made in the USA
Columbia, SC
16 March 2021